— THE CREATIVE BOOK OF —

Papier Mâché

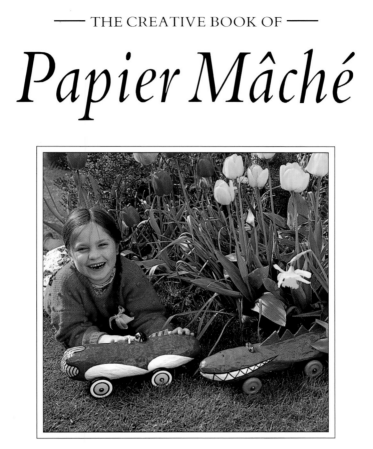

THE CREATIVE BOOK OF

Papier Mâché

Andrew Heaps

Mark & Sue Jamieson

a Salamander book

Published by Salamander Books Limited
LONDON • NEW YORK

Published by Salamander Books Ltd.,
129/137 York Way, London N7 9LG, United Kingdom.

Designed and edited by Anness Publishing Ltd.,
4a The Old Forge, 7 Caledonian Road, London N1 9DX.

© Salamander Books Ltd 1991

ISBN 0 86101 608 4

Distributed by Hodder and Stoughton Services,
PO Box 6, Mill Road, Dunton Green,
Sevenoaks, Kent TN13 2XX.

All correspondence concerning the content of this volume
should be addressed to Salamander Books Ltd.

CREDITS

Editorial Director: Joanna Lorenz

Art Director: Peter Bridgewater

Text Editor: Diana Brinton

Photographer: Zul Mukhinda

Colour origination by: Scantrans Pte, Ltd., Singapore.

Printed in Belgium by: Proost International Book Production.

CONTENTS

INTRODUCTION

A creative medium of immense versatility and charm, papier mâché is now making a long overdue comeback, as artists, craftsmen, and amateurs recognize its potential. The basic techniques are so simple that even relatively young children can master them, and the materials are inexpensive. The end results can either have a very practical application or be purely decorative, and the finishes can range from the naive to the highly sophisticated.

In addition to being very light in weight – which is one reason why it has always lent itself to theatrical uses, from puppets to carnival masks – papier mâché is surprisingly strong and durable. In the past, it was frequently used for trays and even for furniture, such as occasional tables, and in China papier mâché masks have been found that date as far back as the second century AD.

The projects in this book, all illustrated with step-by-step photographs and instructions, demonstrate the techniques used to construct shapes for papier mâché and also show a wide variety of the paint finishes that can be used to decorate the end products. These range from marble and stone effects, created with children's chalks, to highly colourful designs painted in gouache. The finishes are interchangeable, so if you have found the object that you want to make, but you do not like the finish, a glance through the rest of the book should reveal something more suited to your particular needs.

This is an ideal medium in which to let your imagination, creativity and sense of fun run riot, and it is a craft in which the whole family can take part.

— MATERIALS AND EQUIPMENT —

One of the joys of papier mâché is that the materials are so inexpensive, and very little equipment is required. The most expensive materials are those required for the various finishes, and here it would make sense to use what you already possess, before buying anything new.

NEWSPAPER
The basic material is, of course, old newspapers. You will obtain varying degrees of success with different papers, but in general broadsheet papers are of better quality than tabloids.

WALLPAPER PASTE
This is used to paste the layers of paper pieces. Most brands contain fungicide, and are therefore unsuitable for use by smaller children. Non-toxic paste powder can be obtained from craft shops and educational suppliers. To strengthen the mixture, you can add a little white glue.

CARDBOARD
Cardboard is used to provide the basic framework for many of the projects in this book. Unless otherwise stated, the cardboard used is the corrugated variety normally used for boxes, and there is no need to buy it – most shops will be only too delighted to give you as many cardboard boxes as you can use.

Occasionally, objects have been made with thinner card, of the type used for cardboard envelopes or the backs of writing pads. Here again, you will doubtless be able to find suitable cardboard without having to buy it.

MOULDS
In addition to cardboard constructions, papier mâché can also be built up around a mould. Balloons are frequently used for rounded shapes, and ordinary household plates, bowls and other shapes can also be used. In most cases, the papier mâché can be cut or eased from the mould, which can then be cleaned and reused.

In cases such as puppet heads or dolls where a new mould must be created, modelling plastic is used (see page 14). If you are making a particularly large shape, and modelling plastic would be too expensive, clay can be used in the same way.

PETROLEUM JELLY
Moulds are coated before use with petroleum jelly, which acts as a release agent, so that the papier mâché can be removed when dry.

ADHESIVES
White glue – also known as PVA (polyvinyl acetate) or wood glue – is used to glue cardboard and paper pieces together. It is also thinned with water and used as a sealant.

Epoxy glue is used where white glue would not be sufficiently strong. The rapid-setting variety is convenient, and is the type preferred by the authors. It is not, however, suitable for use by children.

An all-purpose or fabric adhesive may be required for attaching ribbons or other decorative pieces of fabric.

TAPE

Brown paper tape is used to hold pieces of cardboard and papier mâché together, and to neaten the edges of cardboard shapes.

Masking tape is not part of the finished construction of a papier mâché shape, but it is useful for holding pieces together while glue dries.

EMULSION AND GESSO

In most cases, a papier mâché shape is coated with emulsion – generally white – in order to prime the surface before decoration. Without this, the colours tend to sink into the paper. The alternative primer is ready-prepared gesso, obtainable from artists' suppliers. This is more expensive, but it provides a thicker layer and has an attractive, soft appearance.

PAINTS AND COLOURS

A wide range of paints and colours can be used to decorate papier mâché. Many of the articles in this book are finished with gouache colours, while others are painted with household paints – gloss or emulsion – and yet others with artists' watercolours. Children's chalks have been used, as have gold felt pens. Acrylics and artists' inks can also be used, and in fact it is worth experimenting with any colouring media that you have to hand.

VARNISH

In most cases, a papier mâché object is varnished, for a hard-wearing and waterproof finish. Acrylic varnish is very clear but it makes gouache colours run, so it is best to use polyurethane, matt or gloss, over these. If the slightly yellowing effect of polyurethane varnish would spoil the look of the piece you can obtain clear varnish, designed for use with watercolours and gouache paints, from artists' suppliers.

OTHER EQUIPMENT

A variety of other items are required. For marking and cutting cardboard and papier mâché shapes you will require the following: pencils (also used to draw motifs on finished objects before painting) and felt pens, a set square, a ruler, a scalpel or utility knife with replaceable blades, a metal straight edge against which to cut, and scissors.

You will also require a large bowl for the paste, and a screw-top jar or other sealable container to hold any paste that is left over.

For painting, you will require artists' brushes for finer details, and houshold painting brushes for coating objects with emulsion and varnish, as well as brush-cleaning materials appropriate to the medium.

———— BASIC TECHNIQUES ————

The basic techniques of papier mâché are very straightforward.
First prepare your work surface, making sure that you have
plenty of space. Ideally, it is best to have a work area where things
can be left between stages.

MIXING THE PASTE

Begin by mixing the paste in a large bowl, following the
manufacturer's instructions (to avoid lumps, sprinkle the powder on
the water and stir; do not attempt to mix water into the powder).
The mixture should be fairly thick. Once it is mixed, leave the paste
to swell, absorbing the water, for about 15 minutes.

If you have to interrupt your work for any length of time, cover
the bowl with plastic food wrap. Have a sealable container, such as a
screw-top jar, so that you can store any unused paste for a little
while, or at least until you have completed all the stages of a project.

PREPARING THE PAPER

The newspaper should be torn not cut, as this produces strips with
softer, and therefore less obtrusive, edges. You will find that it easier
to tear in one direction – along the grain of the paper – than the other.

The size of the pieces will depend to some extent on the size and
shape of the design. If you are making a bowl, for instance, you may
want strips long enough to reach from the centre of the mould up
and over the edge. If the object is an intricately moulded shape, such
as a puppet head, or is very curved, you will achieve a better result
with much smaller pieces. In many of the projects in this book, the
designers have specified the approximate size of the paper pieces.

MAKING A FRAMEWORK

All papier mâché shapes are built up on either a framework or a
mould. If you are using a cardboard framework, the pieces must be
cut out and assembled together. It is important to mark and cut the
cardboard as accurately as possible; use a ruler and set square to draw
right angles, and check squares and rectangles before cutting out by
measuring the diagonals, which should both be the same length.

Paint cardboard edges with white glue and then either hold them
together with masking tape until the glue has dried, or use brown
tape, which can be left in place. (If you are going to be using brown
tape, remember to have a small bowl of water and a sponge beside
you as you work, to wet the tape.) When the framework has been
assembled, neaten the cardboard edges with brown tape before
applying papier mâché.

PREPARING A MOULD

Moulds must generally be coated with petroleum jelly, so that the
papier mâché can be released when dry. It is not generally necessary
to coat moulds made from modelling plastic, however, as this
contains a certain amount of oil.

APPLYING THE PAPIER MÂCHÉ

Use your hand to smear paste on either side of the paper, then ease
away any excess with your fingers before pasting it to the mould. It
is sometimes a good idea to leave pasted strips around the bowl for a
little while to absorb the paste before you apply them.

Apply each successive layer of strips at right angles to the last, in order to avoid creating obvious lines. In most cases, the papier mâché should be left to dry between layers, and this makes it easier to see exactly which areas you have covered when you are applying the next layer. Sometimes, however, several layers can be applied in one session, without waiting for each to dry individually.

JOINING PIECES
In many cases, a finished item consists of papier mâchéd pieces joined either to other pieces of papier mâché or to cardboard (see pages 17 and 34). In these cases, the adjoining edges are painted with white glue and then held together either with brown tape or – only until dry – with masking tape. The join is then concealed by a couple of layers of papier mâché.

DRYING
If you can, dry your papier mâché in the airing cupboard or warm place, standing the object on a cake rack. The drying process can take several days, but it is essential to make sure that the papier mâché is completely dry before moving on to the next stage – to seal in dampness could have a disastrous effect.

SANDING AND SEALING
Depending on the desired end effect, papier mâché can either be coated with emulsion and then painted, or first sanded and sealed before the emulsion is applied. The latter provides a smoother surface when a sophisticated painterly effect is required.

PRIMING
To prepare the finished surface for painting, it is first coated either with gesso or with emulsion; this is generally white, though you could use a darker colour, depending on the colours that you intend using for the decoration. Do not worry if the first coat of emulsion looks rather lined and cracked, the second coat will cover up these deficiencies.

PAINTING AND DESIGN
You will find a wide range of finishes in this book. Always allow one coat of paint to dry before you apply the next. If you are painting intricate motifs, and do not wish to risk painting freehand, you can first draw the outlines in pencil on the white emulsion.

VARNISHING
In most cases, unless you are using gloss paints, the decorated article is finished with one or more coats of varnish (see page 9). This not only protects the painted surface but also the papier mâché beneath.

Make sure that you coat the underneath as well as the top surface.

LOOKING AFTER PAPIER MÂCHÉ
Although papier mâché can be very durable, it is vulnerable to damp, however, so if you wish to use your papier mâché vases for fresh flowers it would be advisable to insert a jar or other container to hold the water.

To use for flower arranging insert a glass inside the papier mâché vase. From cardboard, cut one piece 12.5cm (5in) square and four pieces 25 by 12.5cm (10 by 5in). On each long side of the four pieces, mark a point 5cm (2in) up from the bottom and 2.5cm (1in) in. Draw straight lines from the corners to this point and cut as shown, to make angled sides.

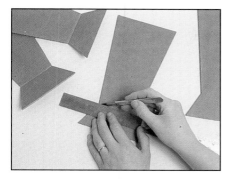

Using a pencil or a medium-sized knitting needle, lightly score across each side piece, from one inner angle to the other. Paint first one side and then the other of all five pieces with white glue. This will seal the card and help to prevent warping.

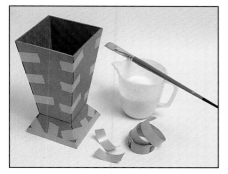

When the pieces are dry, paint all the sides and base edges with white glue. Fit the pieces together as shown, using strips of brown tape to hold them in place. Leave the vase to dry overnight.

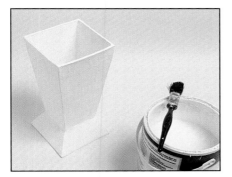

Layering the pieces alternately vertically and horizontally, cover the vase, inside and out, with three layers of papier mâché, each piece approximately 2.5 by 7.5cm (1 by 3in). When dry, sand and then seal with thinned white glue.

Paint the vase all over with white emulsion. The first layer may crack, but when this has dried, apply a second layer, which should be flat and white.

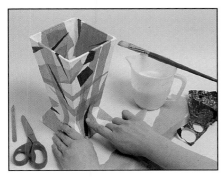

Use the thinned glue to apply pieces of torn coloured tissue paper, inside and out, and then pieces of cut foil sweet wrappers. When dry, apply three layers of acrylic varnish, putting your hand inside the vase for the outer layers, and standing it on its base for the inside. Finish by varnishing the bottom.

P apier mâché is a traditional
material for a puppet head. First,
mould pieces of modelling plastic to
make the components for a Punch
head. You will need the following: a
large ball for the basic head shape, a
large nose, two sausage shapes for
eyebrows, another larger one for the
mouth, a chin, a hat, and a ruff. You
will also need a jam jar to sit him on.

Once you have prepared all the
component parts, assemble them
together, sitting the head on the jam
jar. Do not worry about slight
imperfections and joins – these will be
concealed beneath the papier mâché.

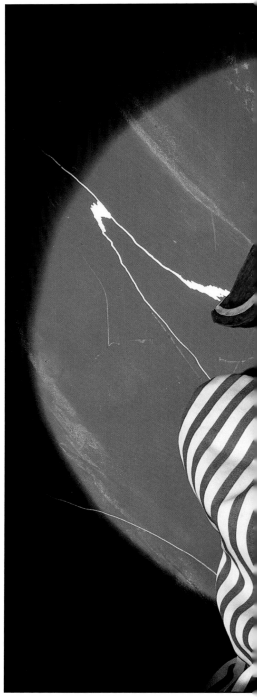

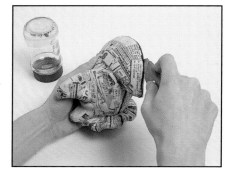

Using thin strips of paper, carefully
papier mâché over the entire head.
Make sure that it is well covered,
giving it from six to ten layers. Leave
it until it has dried out completely.
Remove the head from the jar and
carefully cut the front from the back,
as shown. Cut through the papier
mâché with a craft knife, and then
through the modelling plastic with a
table knife.

Tease the plastic out from the two
halves, taking especial care with the
ruff and the nose. Tape the two
halves back together again and papier
mâché over the join. Give the finished
head two coats of emulsion, then
paint the face, hat and features with
gouache. To make the flesh tint for
the face, add a little red and a touch of
yellow to white. Finish with a coat of
varnish.

With this technique, you can make two attractive wall vases at the same time. First cover a balloon with five layers of papier mâché. When this has dried, pierce the string end of the balloon and remove.

Cut into that end, as shown, gently bending out the resulting teeth. Cover this toothed edge with two layers of 7.5cm (3in) square papier mâché. Allow this to dry overnight, then add a further two layers.

When dry, use a pencil to draw a line dividing the shape into two equal halves. You can erase any unsatisfactory attempts. When you are satisfied, cut along the pencil line with a sharp knife.

Lay each half on cardboard and mark around it, then cut out a back.

Paint the matching edges with white glue, then hold them together with brown tape. Papier mâché the back and edges of each vase, applying three layers over the back and as far inside as you can reach, all at one go. Allow them to dry, preferably on a cake rack in the airing cupboard.

Cut a small hole at the back of each vase, about 2.5cm (1in) down from the top. Sand and seal the vases and give them two coats of emulsion. The vases can then be decorated, either with black and white emulsion, finished with three coats of acrylic varnish; or with gouache, finished with polyurethane.

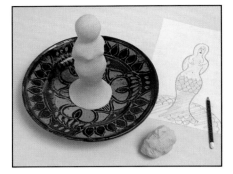

T his mermaid is simply for fun, and is easy to model. Begin by forming a mermaid in modelling plastic. Centre the model on a plate as you work, and keep it very simple – the details can be painted on later. If the plastic is rather stiff, warm it in a low oven for a few minutes to make it more pliable. The plate used has a diameter of 27.5cm (11in) and the mermaid is 22.5cm (9in) high.

Smear petroleum jelly individually over the plate and mermaid. Apply four layers of papier mâché to the mermaid. Apply eight layers of 5 by 32.5cm (2 by 13in) strips to the plate, overlapping the edge by at least 2.5cm (1in). Trim excess, leaving an overhang of 2.5cm (1in) before drying. Make three feet (see page 74), and draw a line around the dry mermaid, as shown.

Cut along the line with a scalpel and ease the papier mâché from the modelling plastic. Immediately – to avoid warping – paint the edges of the cast with white glue; hold them together with masking tape until set, then remove the tape and cover the seam with two layers of papier mâché. Using epoxy glue, fix the feet to the plate.

Glue the mermaid to the plate; place some rolled strips of paste-soaked paper around the join to make a smooth curve and cover with two layers of papier mâché. When dry, sand and seal, then apply two coats of white emulsion. Lightly draw the details in with a pencil. Use gold poster paint for the scales; all the other colours are gouache. Finish with artists' watercolour varnish.

C arnival time! Here is a dramatic mask that can be adapted to fit any number of occasions. Blow up a large balloon and cover with four to six layers of paper pieces, approximately 2.5 by 7.5cm (1 by 3in). When these have dried, draw a mask shape, with eyes and a nose. Use a craft knife to cut out the shape and the holes.

On cardboard, draw a grid of 2.5cm (1in) squares. Copying square for square from the diagram, draw and cut out one beak side, one feather shape and one beak base. Using the beak side as a template, mark and cut a second beak side to make a mirror image pair.

Paint white glue along the edges of the beak pieces and secure them with brown tape. Allow the beak to dry, then attach it to the face in the same way.

Using the feather already cut, mark and cut three more feathers from cardboard to make two mirror image pairs, as shown.

Using epoxy glue, attach the feather pieces to the mask, then apply from two to three layers of papier mâché to the entire mask and leave to dry. When dry, paint the mask with two successive coats of white emulsion.

When the emulsion is dry, coat the mask with red gloss house paint. Allow this to dry before adding either lines of yellow gloss or a decoration of your choice. To complete the mask, make a hole at either side and thread these with black elastic, securing this with knots at the back.

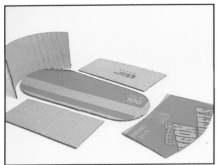

P apier mâché is an ideal medium for this type of toy because it is reasonably strong and very light. First blow up a balloon to a diameter of about 17.5cm (7in) and give it from four to six layers of papier mâché. Cut a base and the four side pieces from cardboard.

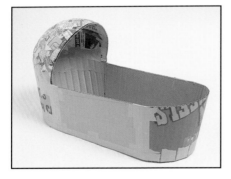

Gently curve the ends to fit the base piece, then use brown tape to fit the pieces together, making a shape similar to an old-fashioned hip bath. Take the balloon and cut a large segment from the fat end. Tape this to the base to make the hood. When cutting the balloon, hold it to the crib and mark around; the segment can be flexed a little to make it fit.

Cover the entire crib with six layers of papier mâché. For the rim, roll half sheets of newspaper into long lengths and tape these around the edge, then papier mâché over this. Make the bottom edge in the same way. Give the entire crib, inside and out, two coats of white emulsion. Paint the outside with light blue gloss house paint, and the inside and rims, top and bottom, with cream gloss.

The basic shape can, of course, be adapted in a wide variety of ways. Draw a mask shape on cardboard. If you want both sides to be exactly the same, draw one side only on stiff paper; cut this out, then draw around the eye and the outside, flipping it over to complete the mirror image. Cut the shape out, then gently curve it to fit the shape of the face.

To make the big nose, blow up a small balloon and cover it with four layers of papier mâché. When this has dried, slice off the end with a craft knife and remove a curved notch from one side to make room for your nose. Tape the nose to the mask, with the notch at the bottom. Make a small hole at either side of the eyes to take the elastic at a later stage.

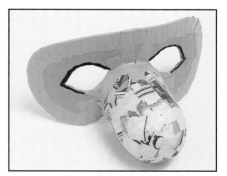

Give the entire mask three layers of papier mâché, and follow this with two coats of white emulsion. Using gouache colours, paint the nose red and the mask black, adding a fine red line around the edge. Finish with two coats of semi-matt polyurethane varnish. To complete the mask, thread black elastic through the holes; adjust to fit, and then make knots behind the holes.

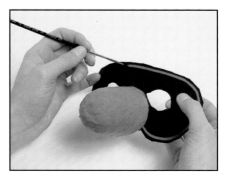

T his antique-style shelving unit makes a charming showcase for small ornaments. The main frame of the shelves is made from cardboard. Cut twelve pieces measuring 35 by 7cm (14 by 2¾in) and six pieces 40 by 7cm (16 by 2¾in). The shelves and sides are all made from three layers each, fitted together as shown and held with brown tape.

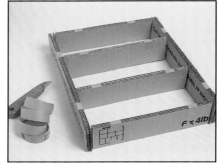

Once the parts are roughly taped together, go over them again with brown tape, covering all the joints and edges. This gives a better finish.

Measure the length of a shelf front and the top. Make paper templates for a shelf fill and scroll top. Using a craft knife, cut three shelf frills (these are used singly) and three scrolls (joined together, like the shelves).

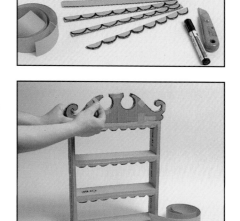

Again with brown tape, add the break-top scroll and shelf frills to the unit.

Laying the unit on cardboard, mark and cut out a back piece. Attach this with white glue and brown tape. For greater stability, add a base, again using three thicknesses of cardboard. Cut the base pieces 1cm (⅜in) wider and 2cm (¾in) longer than the existing base. Also, for fun, glue three table tennis balls to the top. Apply six layers of papier mâché.

When dry, give the unit two coats of emulsion and leave it to dry. Paint with yellow ochre gouache and then add the lines in alizarin crimson. To complete the unit, give it two coats of mahogany-stained varnish. Further coats will give a progressively darker effect, if desired.

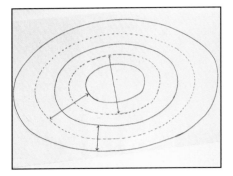

T he basic dish is made by combining three ovals, shown here marked out on a sheet of newsprint. The straight lines indicate the dimensions of the three pieces. The dashed lines are drawn freehand between them. The dishes used for these ovals measure 62.5 by 45cm (25 by 18in), 50 by 32.5cm (20 by 13in), and 29 by 20.5cm (11½ by 8¼in).

Using a sharp point or a ballpoint pen, mark the three shapes on cardboard – a large packing box could be used. Cut them out with a craft knife or scalpel. Using white glue, assemble the pieces as shown. Add strips of masking tape to hold them together while the glue sets. When it has dried, remove the masking tape and cover all the joins with brown tape.

To make the feet, cut three rounds from thin card, using a small cup as a template. Cut a slit from the centre to the edge of each circle and form it into a cone. Secure each cone, inside and out, with brown tape. Seal the dish with thinned white glue. When dry, apply three layers of papier mâché, all at one go, to both dish and feet.

When both are dry, fix the feet to the dish with epoxy glue. Cover the joins with rolls of paste-soaked paper. Smooth over these rolls with two layers of papier mâché. When dry sand and seal the dish, then apply two coats of white emulsion. The pattern is first drawn with a pencil and then painted with two coats of black emulsion. Finish with three coats of gloss acrylic varnish.

To make this clock, you will require a clock movement with a screw fitting behind the hands, available from craft shops. The top and base are octagons, made by trimming the corners from 20cm (8in) squares of cardboard; the side pieces are all 25cm (10in) high, cut to the width of the octagon sides. Cut crenellations into the top edge of the side pieces. Cut a circle from the base.

Tape the pieces together as shown, taping the circle that was cut from the base to the front, to become the clock face.

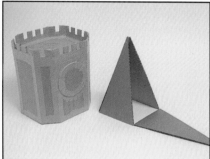

To make the spire, cut four isosceles triangles, with a base of 9cm (3¾in) and a height of 20cm (8in).

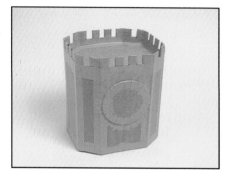

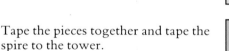

Tape the pieces together and tape the spire to the tower.

Apply six layers of papier mâché. When dry, give the tower two coats of emulsion and then a coat of sand-coloured gloss paint. Dry-brush a dark brown gloss over the sand to create the stony look. Make a hole in the front and fit the clock movement, adding the hands once this is secure. Paint the numerals, winding the hands round to see where they should go.

This mock-baroque cherub is a comical and appealing ornament. Draw an outline of a cherub on a piece of cardboard.

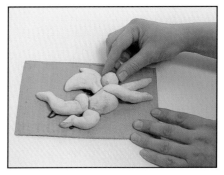

Using balls and sausages of modelling plastic, and keeping to the outlined shape as closely as possible, model a cherub. The shape should be fairly smooth, but small irregularities will be covered by the papier mâché. Papier mâché the cherub. Use small strips to fit around the intricate shapes, and apply from four to six layers. Leave the shape to dry thoroughly.

Carefully cut the modelling plastic and papier mâché away from the cardboard. Very carefully, ease the plastic away from the papier mâché mould. Put the cherub on a piece of cardboard and draw around the shape. Cut out the cardboard shape to use as a back plate, taping it to the back of the cherub. Papier mâché over the tape.

Apply two coats of emulsion, then paint the body in flesh-coloured gouache (white with a touch of red and a little yellow). Paint the wings gold. Draw the features in felt tip, then paint them: eyes white, with black pupil and blue iris (a spot of white for a highlight will bring them to life), and red for the lips. Finish with polyurethane varnish.

A horn of plenty, or cornucopia, is a symbol of abundance or fruitfulness. Cut thin card, such as that used for strong card envelopes, into long strips, about 12mm (½in) wide. Tape these together to make very long strips. Take the longest strip and wind it into a circle about 15cm (6in) across, taping the outer end to hold it. Gently ease out the inside of the circle, to make the body of the horn.

Repeat the process, adding more spirals as necessary, until you have reached the pointed end of the horn. As you work, tape inside and out to hold the shape. It takes time and patience to achieve a good shape, but the result is very satisfying. Give the finished shape six layers of papier mâché.

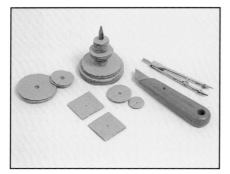

To make the base, cut a large number of circles, graded in size, from cardboard. Using a pencil, push a hole through the centre of each. Putting some large circles at the base, for solidity, slot the rest over the pencil in any order you choose. Keeping the pencil in position, apply papier mâché.

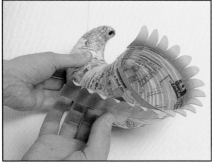

Cut a long strip of card 2.5cm (1in) wide. Draw petals down one side and cut out. Curve each petal, and then tape the strip around the edge of the horn. Position the horn on the base and fix with epoxy glue. Remove the pencil when the glue has dried. Glue a wooden bead to the end of the horn; apply two coats of emulsion, then pick up your paint brush and go wild!

M ade with an ordinary mirror
tile, this would be ideal for a
hallway. Instead of emulsion, the
white ground of the frame has been
painted with gesso to add textural
interest. Cut eight pieces of
cardboard, each measuring 30 by
40cm (12 by 16in). Cut windows from
each, as shown in the diagram,
discarding all the centres except for
the largest.

Firmly tape all the pieces together around the outer edge. Give the resulting frame four layers of papier mâché and leave it to dry.

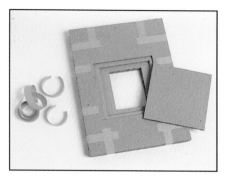

Using a quarter of a broadsheet each time, crumple nine pieces of paper and leave them in paste overnight. Squeeze out the excess paste and form them into sausages, pointed at each end. When dry, after several days, cut each in half with a breadknife, making 18 points of slightly varied sizes.

Using epoxy glue, fix the points around the frame, spacing them evenly. Work on one edge at a time, supporting the frame so that the edge on which you are working is horizontal. When you have finished, leave the glue to harden before decorating the frame.

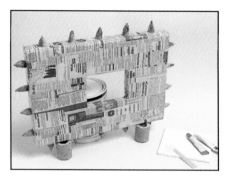

Paint the frame with five layers of ready-prepared gesso. Draw the surface lines with a pencil, and then paint lines on the front and the edges with three coats of gold poster paint. When this has dried, apply a coat of matt polyurethane varnish, giving the white a slightly aged quality.

When the varnish has dried, place a 15cm (6in) mirror tile in the back of the frame. You may need to back it with a piece of cardboard the same size. Finally, fix the spare cardboard window over the tile, using epoxy glue to hold it in place. Brass eye screws can be used for hanging the frame.

T his elegant decorative jug is
    painted with a 1950s-style
design. To make it, papier mâché a
balloon, mark the bottom (a reel of
brown tape was used here), and cut
out the section to create a flat base.

Supporting the balloon shape in a
bowl and using strips approximately
5 by 15cm (2 by 6in), cover the hole
with four layers of papier mâché,
applied at one go. Leave the shape to
dry overnight.

Standing the shape on its base, mark the top of the jug by holding a bowl over the top, placing it at a slight angle. To make the lip of the jug, first cut a triangle of paper and make a fold down the centre. Hold this nose shape against the jug, and mark the profile of the jug on the paper. Trim and fit until the two sit together easily.

Use the template to cut a card lip, adding tags as shown, and cut a corresponding notch from the jug. Sketch a handle for the jug. Cut one from cardboard, making adjustments for a good fit as necessary, then cut three more identical handles from cardboard. From thin card, cut two more handles, with tabs at either end.

Glue and tape the handle together; hold it to the jug; mark the top and bottom, then cut slits and push the tabs through, gluing them to the inside with epoxy glue (use a pallete knife for the lower tags). Also attach the lip. Hold with masking tape until the glue has dried.

When the glue is dry, remove the tape and apply three layers of papier mâché, all at one go, to the handle and the lip, covering all tags. Sand and seal the jug, then apply two coats of white emulsion.

Draw the pattern in pencil and then paint with gouache, starting with the palest shade and ending with black. Finish with a coat of matt polyurethane varnish.

T his durable, papier mâché chocolate box would make a lovely gift. Using a ruler and set square, mark and cut the following pieces from cardboard: four 27 by 15cm (10¾ by 6in), and two each measuring 23.5 by 11.5cm (9¼ by 4½in), 5 by 25cm (2 by 10in), and 5 by 12.5cm (2 by 5in). Glue and tape the largest pieces into two pairs and the narrow strips into a rectangle.

Glue the walls of the box to the base. Hold them with masking tape until the glue has set, then remove the masking tape and reinforce all joins with brown tape. Join the remaining two pieces with glue and tape, then centre them on the lid. Use the blunt end of a pair of kitchen scissors to ease the brown tape into the joins.

Using 5 by 10cm (2 by 4in) pieces, papier mâché both the box and lid, applying three layers. Dry the pieces on a cake stand in the airing cupboard. Lightly sand them and then apply two coats of white emulsion.

Paint the insides of the box and lid with blue gouache, made up to the consistency of thick pouring cream. Draw the outer lines in pencil first, then go over them with a waterproof black felt-tip pen. Do not worry about slight irregularities – they add to the effect. Apply one coat of polyurethane varnish.

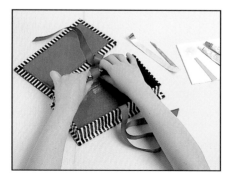

Apply a further three coats, this time of gloss acrylic varnish (painted directly over gouache, it would make the colours run). When this has dried, the ribbon can be fixed in place with epoxy glue. Cover the join with heart shapes cut from adhesive-backed silver paper strip.

This attractive frame is designed to hold a standard 10 by 15cm (4 by 6in) print. From cardboard, cut pieces as shown in the diagram.

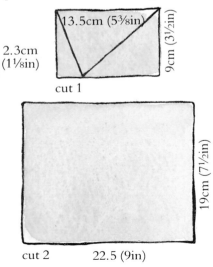

13.5cm (5⅜in)

2.3cm (1⅛in)

9cm (3½in)

cut 1

cut 2   22.5 (9in)

19cm (7½in)

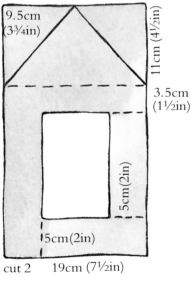

9.5cm (3¾in)

11cm (4½in)

3.5cm (1½in)

5cm(2in)

5cm(2in)

cut 2   19cm (7½in)

Using white glue and brown tape, sandwich the two front pieces and then the two back pieces together. Attach the support to the back of the frame, checking that the angle will be correct when the frame is standing, and that it will not lean too far back. Seal with thinned white glue to avoid warping.

Attach string to the front of the frame with epoxy glue. The three bobbles at the bottom edge are made from crumpled balls of masking tape.

Give the front and back each three layers of papier mâché, pushing the paper carefully around the string. To avoid warping, peg the front and back together when they are almost dry.

When both pieces are fully dry, sand the back and the back of the frame front, and give them two coats of emulsion. Joining the back and front together, apply two layers of papier mâché down the sides and along the lower edge.

Sand, seal and emulsion the finished frame. Gold poster paint is used for the gilding, and the remainder of the frame is painted with gouache and then sealed with clear varnish designed for gouaches and watercolours.

T his fruit bowl is based on a wok shape, with a second bowl placed inside. Coat the inside of a wok with petroleum jelly and apply eight layers of papier mâché all at one time. When this has dried, cut around the edge to neaten. Separate the papier mâché shape from the wok.

Repeat the process on a smaller bowl of a similar shape. When dry, mark a line partway down this papier mâché bowl, as shown. Cut, making a shallow bowl.

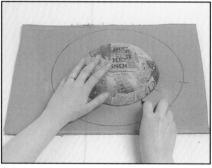

Apply two layers of papier mâché to the edges of both bowls. When dry, mark the wok outline on cardboard, making a register mark on the bowl and the card. Repeat with the smaller bowl, centring it as shown. Cut out the ring and glue and tape the pieces together, aligning register marks. Apply four layers of papier mâché to the rim and leave to dry.

Next apply a layer of tissue paper. This will wrinkle, adding texture. When dry, sand, seal and emulsion the bowl. Using blue and green children's chalks, scribble all over the surface. Brush over the surface with clear water and repeat three more times, to create a greater depth of colour. Finish with a coat of matt polyurethane varnish.

A pair of candlesticks, shaped like pyramids and marbled. From cardboard, cut eight rectangles measuring 17.5 by 10cm (7 by 4in). On one short side of each, measure in 2.5cm (1in) from each corner and mark a line down to the lower corner. Cut as shown, angling all eight rectangles. Also cut four 5cm (2in) squares. Glue and tape the eight pieces into two pyramids.

For each, mark the shape of the bottom on cardboard and cut out. Take a 4cm (1½in) length of cardboard tube, such as the inner tube from a roll of freezer bags. Using scissors, cut 6mm (¼in) nicks at 3mm (⅛in) intervals around one end. Also cut a circle the diameter of the tube from one small square of card, then glue it to a complete square.

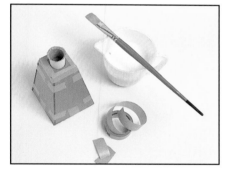

Using white glue and brown tape, fix the bases to the pyramids, then the candle holder tubes into the recessed top pieces. Finally, fix the tops in position. When both candlesticks have been assembled, paint all over with a coat of thinned white glue, to prevent warping.

Cover with three layers of papier mâché, applied all at one go. When dry, sand and seal again with thinned white glue. Apply two coats of white emulsion, then paint with thinned black gouache, adding touches of blue and green while the black is still wet. This overall wash forms the base for the marbling.

Next, apply stronger black lines of gouache, flattening the loaded brush on the edge of the paint pot to shape the end into a chisel. Add more lines with a gold felt-tip pen. Give the candle holder three layers of gold poster paint. Finish with matt polyurethane varnish, brushing along the gold pen lines with light strokes. Give the finished candlesticks a coat of fire retardent.

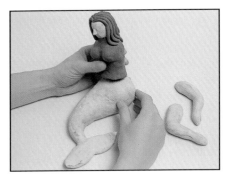

U sing modelling plastic, begin by making the tail, shaping it rather like a whale and curling it up in a lively way. Add an armless torso, and then a round ball for the head. For hair, lay sausages of plastic from the crown of the head to the shoulders. Make the arms from two sausages (check the proportions against the body).

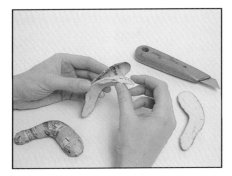

Apply up to six layers of papier mâché to each part. You will have to paper one side first, then turn each piece upside down to complete the process. When dry, cut around the body and each arm and tease out the modelling plastic. Tape the pieces together again and papier mâché over the joins. Apply two coats of emulsion.

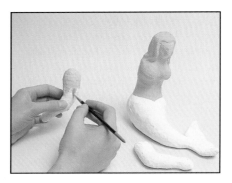

Using gouache, paint the face, torso and arms a flesh colour (see page 13), the hair yellow and the star-fish on each breast orange. Draw the features with felt-tip pens, then paint over them with a fine brush. Use gold poster paint for the tail. Finish with two coats of semi-matt polyurethane varnish.

Thread a chenille needle with thin elastic. Tie a knot in one end and carefully push through one arm, through the body, and out through the other arm. Knot the other end, trimming any excess.

A marbled box with a golden knob on the lid. From cardboard, cut four (side) pieces 15 by 10cm (6 by 4in), two (lids) 13.8cm (5½in) square and two (inside lids) 9cm (3½in) square. Join the sides with white glue and tape, and then mark and cut out a base. Join this to the sides. At the centre of one of the large squares, mark and cut a hole 2.5cm (1in) in diameter.

Glue and tape together the matching squares. Centre the smaller square on the flat side of the larger, and glue and tape it to make the lid (see also page 38). Coat a rubber ball with petroleum jelly and apply four layers of papier mâché, using fairly small pieces. To check for gaps, allow the paper to dry between layers.

Apply three layers of papier mâché to the box at one time, using pieces measuring about 2.5 by 7.5cm (1 by 3in). When the ball is dry, mark the circumference and cut around it.

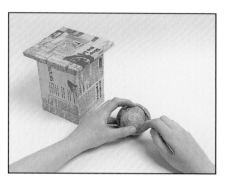

Remove the papier mâché and immediately glue the two halves together, holding them with masking tape. When dry, cover the join with two more layers of small pieces.

Glue the dry ball to the lid recess with epoxy glue. Sand and seal the box and lid, then apply two coats of white emulsion.

Paint the inside of the box and lid with gouache. Decorate the outside with brown and orange chalk, then brush all over with clear water. Repeat two or three times for depth of colour. Give the ball three coats of gold poster paint. Finish with a coat of matt polyurethane varnish.

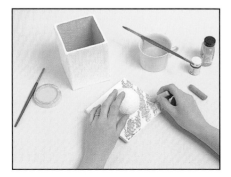

B low up a long balloon, squeezing it so that you have a head-sized lump at one end. Apply six layers of papier mâché, as shown, and leave to dry. Cut two triangles from cardboard, curving the sides slightly to make ears. Tape these to the head end of the balloon and papier mâché over them. Burst and remove the balloon.

Each foot is made from a piece of papier mâché balloon offcut, perhaps left over from a previous project. Cut each foot to the shape of a lemon segment and tape it to the base, bending it to fit. Papier mâché over the joins.

Place the cat on cardboard and draw around the base, including the feet. Cut out the base and glue and tape it to the cat. Papier mâché over the join.

The tail is made from a piece of newspaper, rolled and crunched up and curled around the body. Tape in place and then papier mâché over the tail. When dry, apply two coats of emulsion.

Using gouache, paint the cat black, except for the tip of the tail, the inside ears, the paws and the tummy. Draw the details carefully in pencil, then paint them – eyes yellow with black pupils and white highlights, nose flesh pink, and cheeks white with tiny black dots in rows. Finish with two coats of semi-matt polyurethane varnish.

U sing modelling plastic, make the pieces. The sun is a big blob, with wiggly arms, a nose and eyebrows; the moon is a large crescent with a big nose and eyebrows, and the comet has a blob for a head, a big nose and a flat tail.

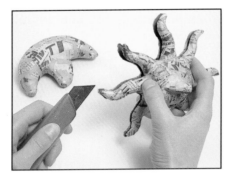

Apply six layers of papier mâché to each shape, covering first one side and then, when that has dried, the other. Mark around the centre of each shape and cut in half.

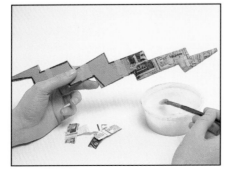

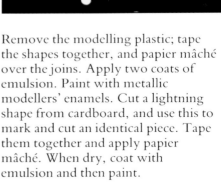

Remove the modelling plastic; tape the shapes together, and papier mâché over the joins. Apply two coats of emulsion. Paint with metallic modellers' enamels. Cut a lightning shape from cardboard, and use this to mark and cut an identical piece. Tape them together and apply papier mâché. When dry, coat with emulsion and then paint.

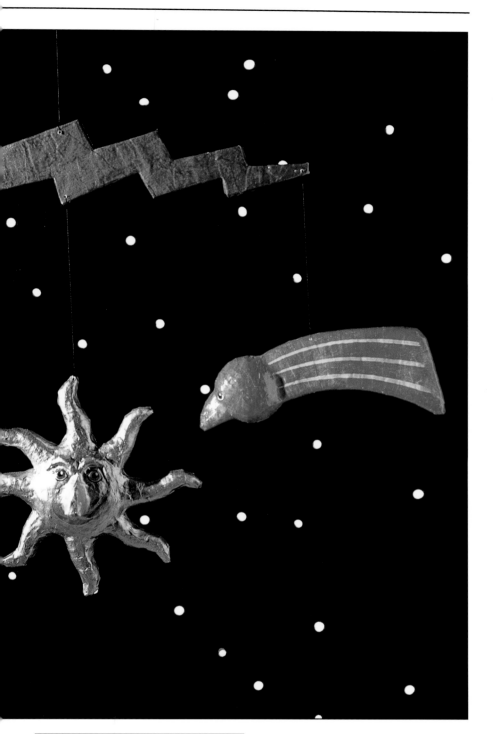

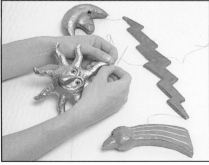

Make holes at the centre top and bottom of the lightning and one at each end. Make a hole at the top of each of the remaining pieces and, using cotton thread, suspend them from the lightning.

B low up a large balloon and apply up to eight layers of papier mâché. Also cover a small balloon. To make each leg, take a large sheet of newspaper and screw it into a long sausage. Now bend it into a loop and tape it to hold the shape. Make each leg slightly different from the others.

Tape the eight legs together. You may use a lot of tape to achieve this, but it will all add to the strength of the finished octopus. Papier mâché over the legs, using long strips of newspaper, dipped in paste and then wound around the legs. You may need to support each leg a little, to prevent the loops from sagging.

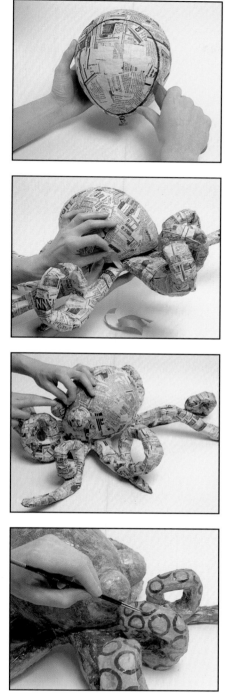

Take the large balloon. Mark and cut an oval on one side, as shown.

The larger round sits in the middle of the tangle of legs, to make the body. Tape it in position, and then papier mâché over the join.

Take the small balloon and cut it in half to make the two eyes. Tape them in position and again papier mâché over the joins.

Apply two coats of emulsion, and then go wild with the colours. This octopus was stippled with green and orange household gloss paint, thinned with white spirit. The maroon suckers were painted with modellers' enamel. The eyes were carefully painted yellow and black, with a green rim.

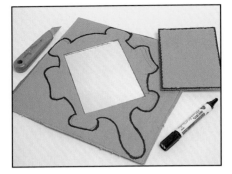

Take a mirror tile and draw the outline on tracing paper. Fold in half down the centre, and draw a mirror outline, framing the tile shape. Draw an inner frill, smaller than the tile size. Cut out and unfold, to make a paper template. Use this to cut a mirror shape from cardboard. Cut out a hole the size of the tile.

Cut two more cardboard mirror shapes, one for the back and one for the front. On the front section, mark and cut out the frill shape. Neaten this inner edge with tape, then paint the edge and around the frill shape with white emulsion. This is because a little of the inside of the mirror may be reflected in the tile.

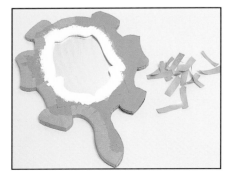

Glue the back and the middle sections together, and glue the tile into its hole. Glue the front to the other two sections, and tape all the way around the sandwich, using small pieces of tape.

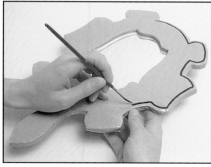

Apply four layers of papier mâché to the entire frame, then give it two coats of emulsion. Paint the frame with mid-blue gloss and, when this has dried, add a line of dark blue, using a fine brush.

Draw a door plate shape on cardboard (you might draw around an existing plate). Draw a simple squiggle down the middle, as shown. Cut the shape out.

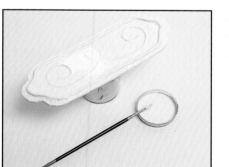

Using sizal, for thickness, glue string around the shape, just inside the edge. Glue thinner parcel string along the squiggle shape.

Using small pieces to maintain as much definition as possible, papier mâché over the string and on the front and back of the plate. Apply up to four layers.

Give the door plate two coats of emulsion and then a coat of light green gloss.

When this has dried, sponge on darker green paint. When dry, lay the door plate on a sheet of newspaper and splash red gloss paint over it, creating a 'Jackson Pollock' effect. Make a hole at the top and bottom, so that it can be attached to the door.

There are many sources you can use for animal badges, ranging from nature books to pastry cutters. When you have chosen your shapes, draw the outlines on cardboard. Using a craft knife, cut out the shapes. Apply four layers of papier mâché to each side.

Using epoxy glue, attach a brooch pin to the back of each shape. Apply two coats of emulsion, then paint the shapes with gouache colours. Add simple black eyes with white highlights. Finish with two coats of polyurethane varnish.

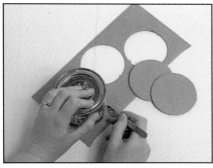

T hese can be decorated in many ways. A tin was used as the template to mark out the cardboard shapes, which were cut out and then painted with thinned white glue before being layered with pieces of paper approximately 5cm (2in) square. Apply four layers to each side, all at one time, covering the edges.

When the coasters have dried, sand and then seal them with thinned white glue. If you intend to paint your coasters and want a pale base colour, apply two coats of white emulsion.

The marbled coasters were painted in the same way as the candlesticks on page 45. The gouache of the black coasters was painted directly on the newsprint. The gold pattern was first drawn with a pencil, and then with a gold felt-tip pen. Look through the book for other possible techniques. Finish with three coats of the appropriate varnish.

T his attractive plant display
column could be brought
outside on a fine day, but is really
intended for indoor use. First, make a
cylinder, 30cm (12in) high and with a
diameter of 15cm (6in), using two
circles and a rectangle of cardboard.
Use white glue and tape to assemble
the cylinder.

Cut two more circles, this time with a diameter of 18.5cm (7½in), and glue them to one end of the cylinder. Make a base from two 22.5cm (9in) squares of cardboard, with side pieces 5cm (2in) high.

For the top, cut a 27.5cm (11in) square of cardboard. Using compasses and leaving 4cm (1½in) at the middle of each side, mark and cut curves from the corners. Bend a length of cardboard along one of the curves. Mark the length of the side, then complete the shape, finishing in a 7.5cm (3in) circle at each end, as shown. Cut four, and assemble as shown.

To fill the gaps at the rounded ends, cut strips of cardboard 4cm (1½in) wide and tape them in position. To finish the top, glue two more 17.5cm (7in) squares to the top of the column. Cut two 27.5cm (11in) squares of cardboard and join them with sides 6cm (2½in) high. Add this to the base of the column.

Cover the column with six layers of papier mâché, not forgetting the bottom, and then apply two coats of emulsion.

Paint to suit your decor. This particular column was painted with pink wood primer, which gave it an attractive matt finish. It was then stippled with a piece of screwed-up rag soaked in dark grey wood primer.

O ne really needs at least two egg cups, so it is sensible to make several at a time. For each cup, first hard boil a large egg. When this is cold, set the pointed end into some modelling plastic, leaving the rounded end uppermost. Apply six to eight layers of papier mâché to this end, covering half the egg.

Remove the egg – don't worry if the shell adheres to the paper. Make the bases from modelling plastic, shaping them rather like dumbells and making them larger at the bottom than the top. Remove the shell shapes and cover each base with six to eight layers of papier mâché. Place each base upside down as you work, so that the bottom is covered.

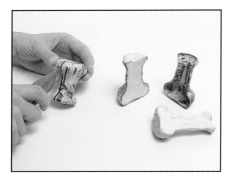

Cut the base in half and remove the modelling plastic. Tape the pieces together, then trim the top so that the cup sits well in it. Glue the cup to the base, and papier mâché over the join. If the rim of the cup is uneven, lay fine sandpaper on a flat surface and carefully sand it flat.

Apply two coats of emulsion, then paint the inside of the cup with dark blue gouache. Add the outer lines, using a fine paint brush. Finish with two coats of semi-matt polyurethane varnish.

T his would make an excellent holder for pencils or brushes. Cover your chosen shape – perhaps a plastic cream or yoghurt container – with petroleum jelly. Apply five layers of papier mâché to the outside at one time, using strips measuring about 4 by 15cm (1½ by 6in), setting each new layer at right angles to the last.

When the papier mâché has dried, mark down the centre line on each side. Cut with a sharp knife down the sides but not across the bottom, slightly sliding the blade under the paper to help to release the paper shape.

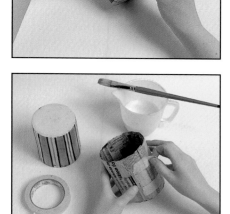

Remove any traces of petroleum jelly with cotton wool and white spirit. Immediately paint the cut edges with white glue. Hold them together with masking tape until the glue has dried. Remove the tape and apply another couple of layers of papier mâché, inside and out.

You could simply bind the edge, but this rolled edge is created with paste-soaked pieces of paper measuring about 7.5cm (3in) square. Work around the edge, holding two of these rolls against the outside edge of the beaker and binding them in place with 2.5 by 10cm (1 by 4in) strips.

When the edge has dried, sand and seal the beaker, and then apply two coats of white emulsion. The pattern was first drawn on the surface with pencil, and then painted with gouache colours. The black lines of gouache were painted last. Finish with a coat of matt polyurethane varnish.

The oranges are the simplest of these colourful ornamental fruits – all you have to do is to papier mâché a small balloon in the normal way. Burst and remove the balloon, covering the end with more papier mâché. When dry, give the shape two coats of emulsion, then paint it with orange gouache. Finish with semi-matt polyurethane varnish.

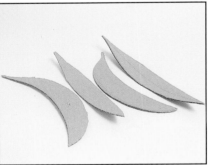

To make a banana, cut out four pieces of card, as shown. Two have curved sides and all are tapered at the top and bottom, and are longer at the stalk end. If in doubt, use a banana skin to make templates.

Bend the sides to fit, and tape them together. Apply four layers of papier mâché and, when dry, two coats of emulsion.

Paint the banana with yellow gouache, blending in a tiny amount of green towards the ends. Paint the stalk and the tip brown. For realism, you might add very thin brown lines partway along the edges, and small spots on each side. Finish in the same way as the orange.

For the pineapple, apply eight layers of papier mâché to a balloon. Cut a long strip of card, about 10cm (4in) wide, and make tapering cuts along it. Curl each leaf shape individually, then tape the strip to the pointed end of the balloon. Start at the centre and work around until you have from four to five circles of leaves. If you need a second strip, make the leaves shorter.

Papier mâché over the join, but not the individual leaves. Apply two coats of emulsion, then paint the leaves with green gouache, made by mixing yellow and blue, so that you can vary the tones from leaf to leaf. Paint the body with honey-coloured emulsion.

You may find it best to draw the segment lines in pencil before painting them, using a fine brush and light brown gouache. Build up the rest of the pattern with orange, sand and brown. It helps if you have a real pineapple to study as you work. The painting is repetitive but well worth the effort. Finish in the same way as the orange.

Y ou will require three fairly large pieces of modelling plastic for this, so that you can make a boat shape, a rectangular block for the boat house, and a roof.

Assemble the three pieces firmly together and place them on a piece of cardboard.

Apply eight layers of papier mâché, making sure that you push the pieces into the corners to maintain the shape. Use the blunt edge of kitchen scissors or something similar to help you to ease the pieces into position.

When the ark has dried, use a craft knife to cut it away from the cardboard. Cut around the boat, from one end to the other; use a craft knife for the papier mâché, then use a table knife to cut the modelling plastic. Remove the plastic, and glue and tape the two pieces together. Papier mâché over the join.

Place the boat on a fresh piece of card, and draw around the base. Cut this shape out and glue and tape it in position. Papier mâché over the join. Apply two coats of emulsion, then draw a large slot in the roof. Bear in mind that the slot must be large enough for the money to be shaken out as well as put in. Cut the slot with care, using a craft knife.

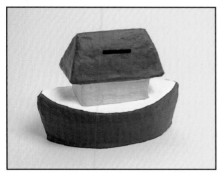

Paint the boat with gouache colours, using brown for the hull, yellow for the deck house, red for the roof and pink for the deck. Give the deck house blue windows and a door, and add blue waves with little white crests around the hull.

A pply eight layers of papier mâché to a large balloon. When this has dried, mark on it a large pointed oval. This will become the cap part of the creation, so if you are making it for yourself, measure your head to get the correct proportions. Also cut two long thin triangles.

Fit the two triangles together into a swallow shape, as shown. Use epoxy glue to hold them together, holding them with masking tape until the glue has dried. Next, glue the swallow shape to the base, again with epoxy. Apply two coats of emulsion, and then paint the swallow shape and the outside of the hat with bright pink modellers' enamel.

Pleat and glue a length of pink tulle under the front edge of the hat, then finish the inside by gluing a piece of soft fabric to the underneath to cover the tulle. To hold the hat in place, you might make a small hole at each side and thread elastic through. Alternatively, use hair clips.

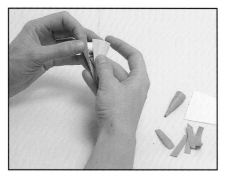

On thin cardboard, draw a circle with a radius of 5cm (2in) and cut out a quarter circle. Bend this into a cone shape and tape over the join. Apply from two to three layers of papier mâché. When this has dried, attach a brooch pin along the length of the shape, using epoxy glue. Make sure that the pointed end of the pin lies at the pointed end of the shape.

Apply two coats of emulsion, then paint with yellow gouache. Add blue spots, then attach a yellow bead to the pointed end of the cone, using epoxy glue. Varnish inside and out with two coats of semi-matt polyurethane varnish. To prolong the life of your flower and hold it in place, pack dampened tissue around the stem inside the cone.

A cheap plastic beach ball, approximately 35cm (14in) in diameter, is used for the base. Coat it with petroleum jelly and then apply six layers of papier mâché all over, using pieces about 7.5cm (3in) square. When the last layer has dried, mark a line around the shape and carefully cut with a craft knife, then remove the papier mâché.

Glue the edges and hold them with masking tape until set, then remove tape and cover the join with two layers of papier mâché. Using a small bowl, mark a circle, large enough for your hand to fit through, on the ball shape and cut it out. Make three large balls (see page 78). When dry, slice a small section from each, so that they can lie flat. Attach the feet around the hole with epoxy glue.

Cover the base with black tissue paper, torn into squares of approximately 10cm (4in). Paint one side of the paper and apply this side to the lamp, overlapping pieces slightly. Give the feet three coats of poster paint, and then paint the entire base with matt polyurethane varnish. Finish with fire retardent, available from theatrical suppliers.

Using a craft knife, make two more holes in the base – one at the top for the light fitting, and one about 2.5cm (1in) away from the hole at the bottom, to carry the flex. When you wire the lamp, fit a cord grip inside the lamp to secure the flex.

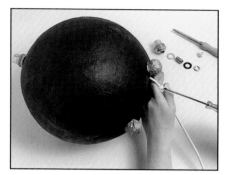

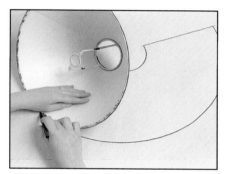

For the shade, it is simplest to use an existing shade to make the pattern. Mark the outline on thin paper, such as newspaper. Cut this out and place over the existing shade to check for fit. When you are satisfied, mark the outlines on thin cardboard or thick cartridge paper, making sure that there is a sufficient crossover.

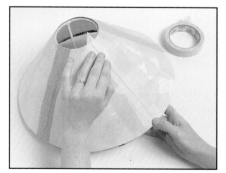

Tear tissue paper into 10cm (4in) squares and apply it to the cardboard – the pencil outlines will still be visible through the paper. Pink tissue paper was used first, and these were overlaid with strips of blue and yellow, to create purple and orange tones. Cut out the shade and hold it over a lighted lamp – add more pieces if needed (we added some black).

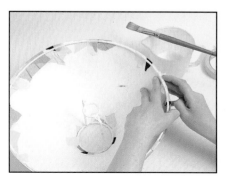

Paint the overlapping edges with white glue; hold with masking tape until dry. Using new supports or those from the old shade, attach them with white glue, having first given them a coat of white emulsion. Treat the finished shade with fire retardent, available from theatrical suppliers.

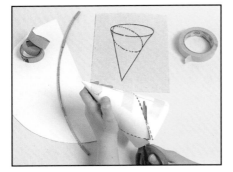

F rom thin cardboard, cut circles
40cm (16in) in diameter, then cut
these in half. Form each semicircle
into a cone, making some tighter than
others, and hold with masking tape.
Trim the excess, as shown, then
replace the masking tape with brown
tape. For each stem, cut three lengths
of galvanized wire and bind with
brown tape.

Apply three layers of papier mâché to
each cone, inside and out, and wrap
strips around the stems. Working
freehand, draw long leaves; cut them
out and then apply papier mâché.
Stand the cones on their top edges to
dry, to curve the points. The leaves
can be dried over various objects, to
shape them. When dry, trim each
cone, making a hole for the stem.

Insert a stem into each cone for about
12mm (½in). Place a paste-soaked
newspaper ball over the stem to hold
it. Smooth the ball to the sides of the
cone. Bind cone and stem on the
outside with five layers of pasted
strips, making a natural-looking
bulge at the top. Dry upside down,
with the stem leaning against a
support. When dry, sand and seal and
apply three coats of emulsion.

The green for the leaves and stems was made by mixing brilliant green gouache with spectrum yellow, zinc white and a touch of spectrum red. When you reach the bulge of the stem, start to add more white, fading the green into the white of the flower. (You might practise on paper.) Coat the stems and leaves only with matt polyurethane varnish.

DRAMATIC EARRINGS

The fixings for these can be bought at bead shops. The balls for the earrings are made from broadsheet newspaper, crumpled up and left in paste to soak overnight. The three sizes are made from a half, a quarter, and an eighth of a page respectively. When soaked, squeeze out excess paste and shape them into firm balls. Leave to dry.

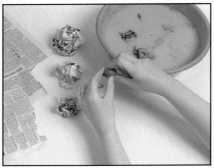

Use a hat pin or similar sharp point to make holes for the connecting hooks of the dangling earrings: one hook for the largest ball, and one at both the top and bottom of the middle and small sizes. Use epoxy glue to secure the hooks. For the clip-on earrings, make one large ball, then cut it in half when dry.

Make indents for the glass jewels with a countersinking tool. Paint the dangly earrings with black emulsion and the gold ones with poster paint, finishing the latter with polyurethane varnish. Use a matchstick to put a drop of white glue in each indent, and push in a glass jewel. Connect up the dangly earrings and fit the ear wires. Attach clips to the other pair with epoxy glue.

S mear the inside, the edge and about 2.5cm (1in) down the outside of the chosen bowl or bowls with petroleum jelly. This relatively small bowl was given six layers of papier mâché all at once. The paper strips should be long enough to run from the inside centre of the bowl, up the side and over the edge, and should slightly overlap.

When completely dry, twist the papier mâché slightly and remove it from the mould. Trim the edges, and clean away traces of petroleum jelly with cotton wool and white spirit. Using small pieces of papier mâché, neaten the cut edge of the bowl. When this has dried, sand and seal the bowl and apply two coats of white emulsion.

The underwater motifs were drawn on the emulsion in pencil, and two coats of a watercolour wash – a mixture of blue and green – was then applied. The colours separate and run into the paper, but this just adds to the subtlety. The motifs, which are still visible through the wash, are then filled in with gouache.

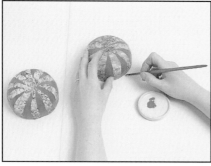

When the inside of the bowl has dried, paint the outside in the same manner. Touches of gold poster paint can then be added to the design and to the rim. Finish with clear varnish, of the type designed for use with watercolours.

C ut a circle from thin card – a lampshade with a diameter of 40cm (16in) was used as a template. Cut a slit from the centre to the edge of the card and form it into a cone – the large overlap will help to strengthen the shape.

Hold the cone together with masking tape, and mark the base circle on cardboard. Make register marks on the cone and the circle, then cut out the circle. Hold the circle to the cone with masking tape, aligning register marks. Mark a central line around the cone, dividing it into two equal halves. Using a craft knife, cut it in half.

On cardboard, mark a triangle to fill the empty side of each half-cone. Cut out the triangles. For each book end, fill a plastic bag with about 750g (1½lb) of sand. Knot the bag, put it inside the shape, then put the triangular back in place. Replace all masking tape with brown tape, and seal the cardboard. Apply three layers of papier mâché.

When dry, sand and seal the bookends, and paint with two coats of white emulsion and then with yellow gouache. When this has dried, cut shapes from kitchen foil and glue them in place. Give both bookends a coat of matt polyurethane varnish, then cut circles from fun-fur fabric, and attach these with fabric glue.

T his decorative column is based on one seen in Savannah, Georgia. Start by drawing the shape, which measures approximately 25 by 52.5cm (10 by 21in) on a drawing board. Roll out a clay sausage about 2.5cm (1in) thick, and press it along the line, flattening the base to make the roll D-shaped. Coat the shape and 5cm (2in) of board on either side with petroleum jelly.

All at one go, apply four layers of 10cm (4in) square papier mâché (you may require smaller pieces on inner curves). The vertical lines are made from lengths of semicircular wooden dowel, sanded into rounds at each end. These are simply given two coats of white emulsion. When dry, cut the papier mâché from the board and remove the clay. Clean the flat edges with white spirit.

Sand and seal the surface, and apply two coats of emulsion. Draw a line 6mm (¼in) out from the raised surface and trim away the excess. Position the pieces on the wall with masking tape and draw around them. Take them down and apply impact adhesive to the column pieces and the wall, then fix them in place, filling any gaps with ready-mix plaster.

S mear the surface and well over the edges of your chosen plate with petroleum jelly. Placing each layer at right angles to the last and using strips 5cm (2in) wide, apply eight layers of papier mâché all at one go. Trim the irregular edge to leave a 2.5cm (1in) overhang, and leave it to dry. Also make three small balls (see page 78).

When dry, remove the papier mâché from the plate and trim the edge to shape. Using white spirit and cotton wool, remove any traces of petroleum jelly. The plate seen here was slightly warped, giving it a curving shape, but we decided that this only added to its charm! Neaten the edge of the plate with small pieces of papier mâché.

When the balls are completely dry, which can take two days in the airing cupboard, cut a small piece from one side of each, to give it a flat surface to lay against the plate.

Attach the feet to the back of the plate. It is a good idea to hold them in position first with masking tape, to check that they are evenly spaced. Apply epoxy glue and again hold the feet in place with masking tape until the glue has dried. Sand and then seal the plate, before giving it two coats of white emulsion.

Lightly draw the pattern on the plate with a pencil, then paint on a wash of pale blue watercolour. The pencil marks will show through, and the pattern can then be painted in gouache colours. When the paints have dried, finish with one coat of watercolour varnish, available from artists' suppliers.

RIMMED BOWL

You could make feet for this rounded bowl, but it looks very decorative lying on its side. Start by applying six layers of papier mâché to a balloon. Allow to dry between layers. When dry, remove the balloon and cut around the widest point with scissors. Put the bowl shape on cardboard and mark around it. Make register marks on the bowl and cardboard.

Mark the width of the rim – say 6cm (2½in) – on paper, and use this to mark a second circle outside the first. Cut out the rim and seal both sides of the rim with thinned white glue. Apply white glue to the inner edge of the rim and the edge of the bowl. Fit them together, matching register marks, and hold with brown tape. When dry, neaten and secure the rim in place with more tape.

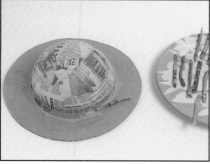

Roll up 7.5cm (3in) squares of paste-soaked paper and fit these around the join on the underside of the rim. Next, apply three layers of papier mâché to both sides of the rim, carrying the layers onto the bowl to smooth over the join.

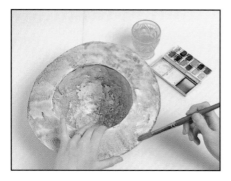

When dry, sand and seal the bowl and give it two coats of white emulsion. Make a watery grey wash by mixing dark brown and dark blue watercolours, then paint the bowl with two coats. The colours will separate a little, creating a stone effect. Finish with a coat of polyurethane varnish. The slightly yellow tone will add to the stone-like look of the bowl.

A pply eight layers of papier mâché to a sausage balloon, drying between layers, then remove the balloon and paper over the hole. Cut two axles – long enough to hold the wheels clear of the body – from dowel. Drill screw holes for the wheels. At one end of the body, mark an outline to carry one axle. Cut, starting small and gradually enlarging the shape. Repeat at the other end.

Paint the edges of the holes and the axles with white glue. Insert the axles and hold them in place with masking tape. When the glue has set, remove the masking tape and cover the axles, where they touch the body, with at least four layers of papier mâché, using strips measuring about 4 by 7.5cm (1½ by 3in).

Add details. The dinosaur's spine ridge is made from cardboard, as are the driver's windscreen and scarf. His head is a large pasted-paper ball (see page 78), and the dinosaur's eyes are smaller balls. Cut a sliver from each ball and glue this flat side in place. Papier mâché over the added shapes.

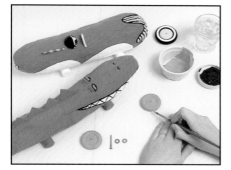

Sand and seal the shape(s), and then apply two coats of white emulsion. Also give the wheels, which can be bought from hobby shops, two coats of emulsion. When this has dried, draw the outlines of any painted pattern or details in pencil.

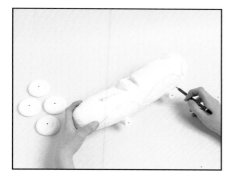

All the colours used here are gouache. Start with the palest, and work up to the darkest colours. It may be simplest to paint in sections, completing the top and then the underside.

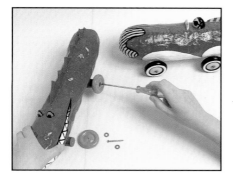

Finish with a coat of clear watercolour varnish, including the wheels. When dry, fix the wheels in position, using a metal washer on both sides. Take care not to make them so tight that they are unable to turn.

S tart by cutting the shapes from thin card: a circle with a diameter of 12cm (4¾in), a tear shape for the head of the bird, and a long triangle for the tail. Make a slit in the circle from the centre to the outside and shape it into a cone. Glue the edges together, and hold the shape with masking tape until this has set.

Glue the head and tail in position, with the pointed ends inside the cone. Again, hold with masking tape until the glue has set. Remove the tape, and cover all joins with brown tape.

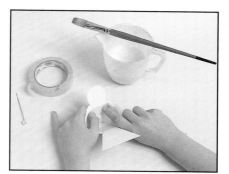

Take a hat pin (the one used here was an inexpensive, pearl-ended version) and push it through the cone, as shown. Add a little epoxy glue to hold it in place. Apply three layers of papier mâché, all at one time. The tail will be floppy when wet, so arrange it to dry in an attractive shape; you might use some form of support, such as a matchbox.

Make a point for the beak (see the points around the mirror, on page 35). Fix the beak in place with epoxy glue. Also make two indents for the eyes, using a countersinking tool (see page 79).

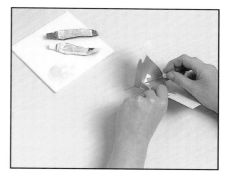

Sand and seal the bird, and then give it two coats of white emulsion. The inside of the bird was painted in rich red gouache, the outside in black and the beak in orange. When the paint has dried, give the bird a coat of matt polyurethane varnish. The spots on the inside are now added, using gold glitter paint.

The final stage is to set jewels into the indents for eyes, using a little white glue on the end of a matchstick. The same basic design would also make a delightful Christmas tree decoration; simply replace the hat pin with a length of thin wire, knotted to prevent it from passing straight through.

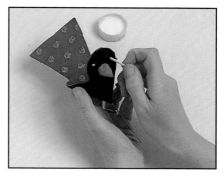

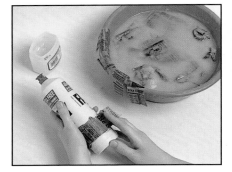

F irst, layer a bowl with papier
mâché (see page 80). To make a
foot ring, coat the lower section of a
bottle, in this case a bottle of washing
up liquid, with petroleum jelly and
apply six layers of papier mâché.
When dry, cut a neat line around the
top and bottom and make a vertical
slit. Remove the ring and rejoin the
edges, using white glue and tape.

For the lid, cut two circles of
cardboard slightly larger than the
diameter of the bowl, and two
slighter smaller, to fit inside the rim.
Cut a 10cm (4in) length of cardboard
tube (the inner tube from a roll of
freezer bags was used here). At the
centre of one of the larger circles,
mark and cut out a circle the
diameter of the tube.

Paint all the lid sections with thinned
white glue. When dry, glue the pieces
together as seen in the picture, fitting
the tube into the hole at the top of the
lid. Cover all edges with brown tape.
Tape the foot ring to the bowl, then
cover this join with papier mâché
strips. Also cover the lid with three
layers of papier mâché.

When dry, sand, seal and emulsion the bowl and lid. Draw the pattern on both pieces with a pencil. Paint the entire lid and the inside of the bowl with two coats of a yellow ochre watercolour wash. Use gouache for the rest of the painting, starting with pale colours and finishing with the darkest. This bowl was finished with watercolour varnish, but polyurethane could be used instead.

INDEX